Contents

Cathy® is distributed internationally by Universal Press Syndicate.

Cathy Twentieth Anniversary Collection copyright © 1996 by Cathy Guisewite. All rights reserved. Printed in the United States of America. No part of this book may be used or reproduced in any manner whatsoever without written permission except in the case of reprints in the context of reviews. For information write Andrews and McMeel, a Universal Press Syndicate Company, 4520 Main Street, Kansas City, Missouri 64111.

ISBN: 0-8362-2523-6

Library of Congress Catalog Card Number: 96-84532

TWENTIETH ANNIVERSARY
COLLECTION

by Cathy Guisewite

Andrews and McMeel
A Universal Press Syndicate Company
Kansas City

Other Cathy® Books from Andrews and McMeel

Introduction

When I started *Cathy*:

- ♥ "Pursuing a career" was a new phrase for women.
- ♥ Pasta was called noodles, and was forbidden on diets.
- ♥ Bread was called starch, and was eaten only by thin people.
- ♥ VCR's didn't exist.
- ♥ Answering machines didn't exist.
- ♥ Control-top pantyhose didn't exist.
- ♥ Telephones had dials, were leased from the phone company, and worked.
- ♥ Typing corrections were made with little bottles of white paint.
- ♥ No one ate yogurt.
- ♥ Nothing was low-fat.
- ♥ The American public, in general, weighed ten pounds less per person.
- ♥ All married women used their husbands' last name.
- ♥ The only thing a watch could do was tell time.
- ♥ No one ever went to a restaurant to make her own salad.
- ♥ "Ms." was a typo.
- ♥ Lingerie was something you got at a bridal shower.
- ♥ People added and subtracted on paper.
- ♥ It took forty-five minutes to cook a baked potato.
- ♥ The frozen dinner section was a foot wide and contained pot pies.
- ♥ Everyone drank tap water.
- ♥ Women didn't sweat.
- ♥ Therapy was whispered about.
- ♥ "Skin care" was putting on baby oil before lying in the sun.
- ♥ Extremely urgent, rush documents went by mail.
- ♥ No one had ever heard of cellulite.
- ♥ Motherhood was something your mother did.
- ♥ Every time you bought gas, someone washed your windows.
- ♥ All catalogs contained at least one section of power tools.
- ♥ The only way to get cash was to stand in line at the bank.
- ♥ Nobody worked out.
- ♥ Except for *Brenda Starr* and *Nancy*, all the comic strips starred men.

When I started *Cathy*, women were just beginning to abandon Donna Reed as a role model. It's hard to comprehend how many transformations we've been through since then. How many full self-image makeovers we've undergone, how many dreams we've improved upon, how many new expectations we've embraced, and how many new outfits we've required to be dressed appropriately for each one.

Considering that I can spend up to an hour trying to decide which pair of virtually identical pairs of black shoes to wear, choosing which strips to include in this book was a bit of a challenge.

Do I include the ones I think are funny now, or the ones I thought were funny twenty years ago? Choose strips that reflect my evolution as a confident, enlightened person, or admit to entire years I spent sobbing next to the phone?

I decided to be as honest as I could stand to be, to give enough of a sample of each year so the times sort of roll out in the book the way they did in life . . . to trust that a lot of my readers who are with me now were with me way back then . . . and to know that no matter how many different routes our lives have taken we have shared a pretty amazing trip together.

1976–1980

I drew my first comic strip on the kitchen table in between bowls of fudge ripple ice cream. It wasn't a comic strip, really, just an explosion of frustration that wound up on paper instead of in my mouth.

I was twenty-five years old, forty-five pounds overweight, and living alone in a little apartment in a suburb of Detroit at the exact time in history when the concepts of "woman as adoring, subservient home-maker" and "woman as independent, invincible human being" took up equal, and pretty much constantly clashing, parts of my brain.

It was a confusing time for almost everyone. Women's music was militant. Women's groups were revolutionary. Women's reading material left women either barely able to speak to men or dating all of them at once. The only clear voice of right and wrong was Mom, who began simultaneously cheering for me to conquer the world, and sending clippings reminding me that men preferred women who let them win.

Universal Press Syndicate bought my strip as soon as they saw it, even though it barely resembled a comic strip at that point. They called my art style "primitively energetic," and said my writing was the first they'd seen that was emotionally honest about how women were struggling with change.

I spent every night that followed frantically trying to learn how to draw on a drawing board under the stairway in my apartment, and told no one but my immediate family that I was working on a comic strip.

The first day *Cathy* ran in the paper, I hid in my office in the adver-tising agency where I worked as a writer, praying that no one would read the comics that day.

9

10

12

14

19

20

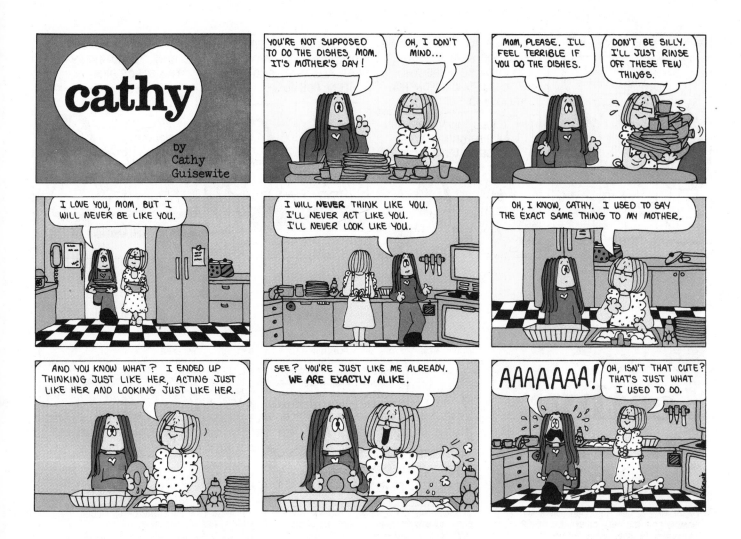

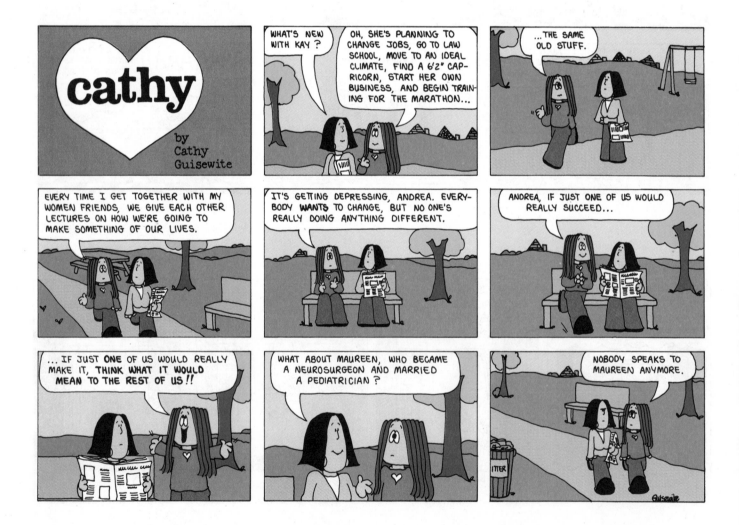

27

28

If the world works, it's because women almost never do anything part way. If we go shopping, we shop until we've tried on every pair of shoes. If we start something, we're guilt-ridden until we finish. If we're responsible for someone, we're responsible until the end of time. If there's an open box of chocolate, there's an empty box of chocolate.

Women are genetically programmed to go for it. My grandmother, in her day, went for it by baking bread from scratch and meticulously hand washing, starching, and ironing four shirts a day for my grandfather. In the early '80s, with the full force of the women's movement cheering us on, my peers and I went for it by flinging ourselves into career potential.

Cathy's an only child in the comic strip, but in real life I have two sisters, Mary Anne and Mickey, who are my role models of compulsion. I never made them characters in the strip because we're so much alike; it's almost as though we're three women with one brain.

I never really created any characters . . . just sort of smashed the various anxieties I was having into different bodies and gave them names.

Andrea, Cathy's best friend, was always the perfect, emotionally unrattled voice of enlightenment, who planned her wedding with the tenacity of an account manager, including slotting a seven-day window of time to meet a husband.

Irving, Cathy's boyfriend, was every problem I'd ever had in a relationship, including the fairly substantial problem of expecting a man to instantly adapt to the latest version of myself I'd created from the last self-help article I'd read.

Mr. Pinkley, Cathy's boss, was the worst of corporate life that I'd experienced, and now that I was my own boss, it turned out, was also the worst in myself as a boss.

The Sales Clerk, who was the same woman in every store and institution Cathy went in, was a symbol of all clashes with bureaucracy. She was also always the same woman because that's the only way I could draw a sales clerk.

Mom and Dad are, thankfully, two people with wonderful senses of humor about themselves.

30

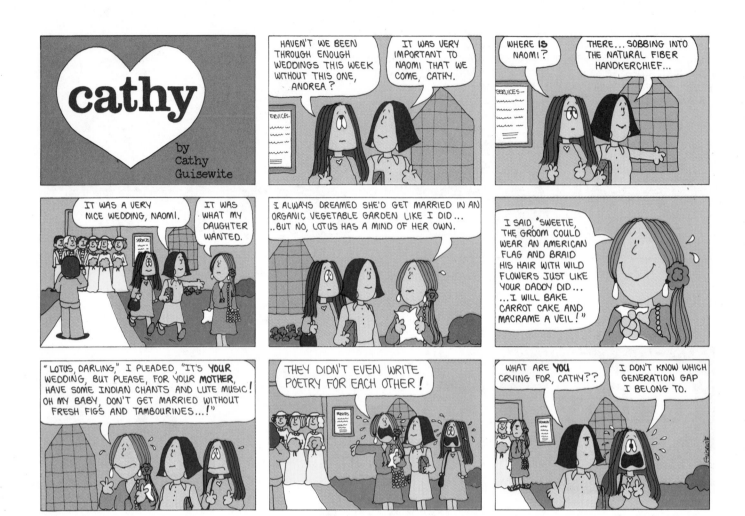

36

37

45

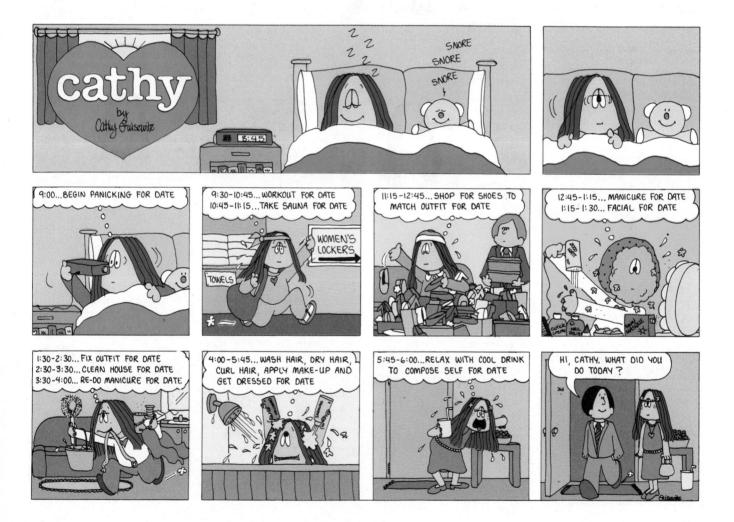

53

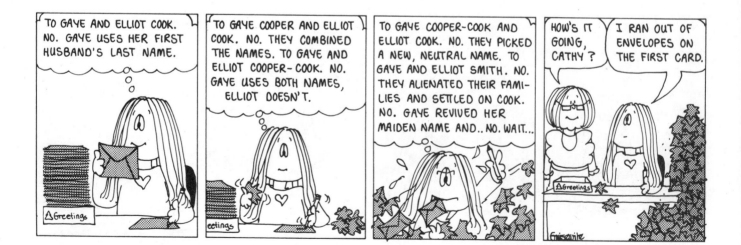

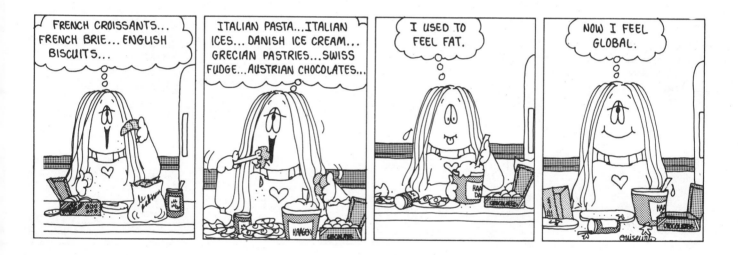

61

62

69

70

My father reads the newspaper. My mother cuts it up with scissors and mails it to people. My father does the task at hand. My mother turns it into a psychotic production. While I think my sense of humor came from Dad, the gene that allows me to obsess about something long enough to turn it into a comic strip definitely came from Mom.

I start every week with the goal of creating something funny, relatable, original, and insightful . . . ideally framing it in such a way that it also becomes a microcosm of some larger, universal truth . . . I like to slide in a bonus joke so if someone doesn't like or get the punch line, they'll be amused by some phrase along the way that will make reading all the other words worthwhile . . .

By 9:30 in the morning, I've usually achieved a state of complete creative paralysis, which moves into a depressed stupor and ends seven days later with me begging my sister, columnist Mickey Guisewite, for help and flinging myself at a Federal Express truck.

In the late '80s, it was pretty much a full-time job to try to make sense of the completely opposite trends that everyone I knew was simultaneously trying to embrace.

We had the rise of the gourmet fattening food industry at the exact same time as the rise of the fitness movement . . . the boom in organic, made-from-scratch cooking at the exact same time as people had four seconds left in the day to cook anything . . . a new environmental awareness at the exact same time that everything in the world was made of and paid for with plastic . . . the launch of the trashy lingerie business at the exact same minute the return to good, old-fashioned values mood was kicking in . . . the height of the self-obsessed, gizmo-filled yuppie years at the exact same time as the call to the simple, selfless joys of parenthood . . .

While Cathy's friends, Andrea and Luke, gave birth to their wonder-baby, Zenith, Cathy ate Belgian chocolate in an aerobics outfit, bought a condominium, and adopted her puppy, Electra.

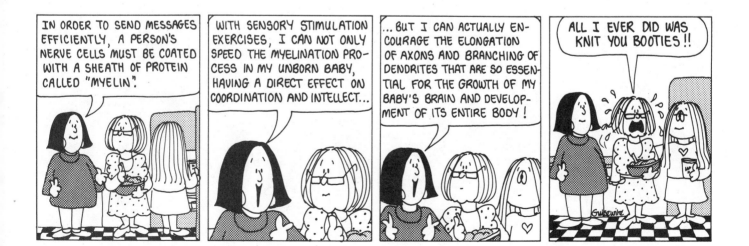

Panel 1: HAVE YOU PAINTED THE BABY'S ROOM YET, ANDREA?

Panel 2: NO, BUT WE **HAVE** BOUGHT BABY'S FIRST ISOKINETIC WORKOUT WAGON... AN ERGONOMIC STROLLER... COMPACT DISC MUSICAL MOBILE... A PC WITH INTERACTIVE, PRE-VERBAL SOFTWARE... A "BUSY BOX" WITH 32-DIGIT AUTO-REDIAL...

Panel 3: CRIB SHEETS PRINTED WITH THE WORKS OF THE 17TH-CENTURY MASTERS.... FLASH CARDS... ENOUGH LEGO SETS TO RECONSTRUCT MANHATTAN... NON-TOXIC MARKERS COLOR COORDINATED WITH BABY'S HAND-LOOMED VCR COVER... AND A STUFFED LEMUR THAT PLAYS THE OPERAS OF PUCCINI!!

Panel 4: HAVE YOU PAINTED THE BABY'S CONDOMINIUM YET?

Panel 5: IS YOUR TV SET TURNED OFF? / YES, THE TV IS OFF, ANDREA. IT'S SAFE TO BRING YOUR UNBORN BABY INTO THE ROOM.

Panel 6: SORRY, CATHY... BUT EXCEPT FOR THE ONE TIME I ACCIDENTALLY WALKED PAST A TV PLAYING SATURDAY MORNING CARTOONS, MY BABY HAS ONLY BEEN EXPOSED TO PBS.

Panel 7: FOR 8½ MONTHS LUKE AND I HAVE SAT TOGETHER AND LISTENED TO HOURS OF FASCINATING EDUCATIONAL PROGRAMS WITH OUR FETUS.

Panel 8: WE CAN'T WAIT TO FIND OUT WHAT ITS WONDROUS NEW MIND HAS RETAINED! / HORDAK! SKELETOR! HE-MAN! FROSTED FLAKES!

Panel 9: FUNNY, ISN'T IT, THAT IT'S US —THE WOODSTOCK GENERATION— WHO ARE LEADING THE WAY IN DRUG-FREE CHILDBIRTH?

Panel 10: ALL THAT TIME OF TAKING DRUGS FOR NO REASON.... AND NOW WE WOULDN'T EVEN THINK OF TAKING AN ASPIRIN!

Panel 11: NOW, WHEN I'M TRYING TO PUSH A SEVEN-POUND HUMAN BEING OUT OF MY BODY, ALL I NEED IS HERBAL TEA, CALMING MUSIC AND...

Panel 12: ...**ETHER!** I WANT **ETHER**!! / EVERYTHING OK? / YEAH, JUST A LITTLE NOSTALGIA.

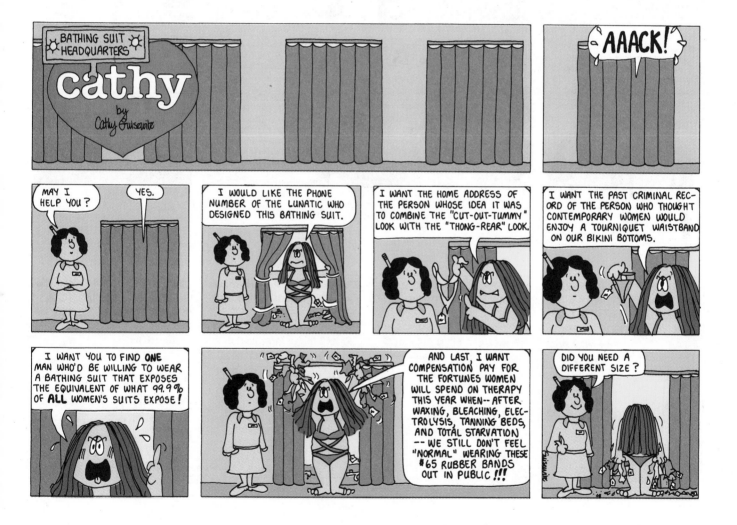

84

91

92

100

102

107

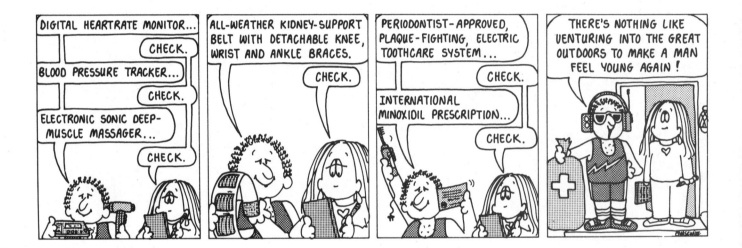

110

In the '70s I thought I'd be a success as a woman if I earned my own way. In the '80s, I thought I'd be a success as a woman if I were the president of a billion dollar company, had a sensitive soul-mate husband, two bilingual children, buns of steel, and a compost heap. In the '90s, I pretty much feel I'm a success if I can get through the afternoon without eating a cheesecake.

What can we say about a decade that includes more women in positions of power than ever before in history, and has already had us dressing in the waif look, the baby doll look, the rubber mini, the transparent slip dress, the padded, pushup bra, sky-high stilettos, apron dresses, bright red lips, and striped hair?

What can we say about a time when people wear cross-training shoes to drive four-wheel-drive off-road vehicles to order a lite burger out of a clown's mouth at Jack-in-the-Box?

How did we go so quickly from women fighting for the right to enter the workplace, to most women working full time as a necessity of life . . . and if we've really come so far, why is it still so hard to find a job that pays more than day-care costs?

I would tap into the global universe of information and answers on the Internet, but in real life, I have a four-year-old daughter who's standing at the door, pleading for me to come play Cinderella with her for the seven thousandth time this evening. She's Cinderella, and I play all the other parts, including the handsome prince, and the part where I get to stand back and watch the next generation of women growing up right in front of me.

For all the people who wonder where I get my ideas, how much do I really need to make up?

OF COURSE THAT LOOKS DRAB. YOU NEED ACCESSORIES!

THE PSEUDO-SILVER CUFFS... THE CHUNKY ERSATZ PEARLS... THE SIMULATED ETHNIC BEADS... THE ARTIFICIAL GOLD CHAINS... THE MOCK-JEWEL EARRINGS...

PUT IT ALL TOGETHER AND SEE WHAT YOU HAVE ??!

THE FAUX-WOMAN.

WITH, I MIGHT ADD, THE BOGUS CREDIT LINE.

NEXT!

"SIXTIES DRESSING WITH A NEW TWIST." WHAT'S THE NEW TWIST?

THE NEW TWIST IS THAT A "FLOWER-POWER" TUNIC NOW COSTS $300!

THE VERY STYLES THAT DEFINED A WHOLE DECADE OF REBELLION AGAINST CAPITALISM ARE NOW BEING CHARGED ON EX-HIPPIES' PLATINUM AMERICAN EXPRESS CARDS FOR $300 A POP!

AMERICA IS ALIVE AND WELL! LONG LIVE AMERICA!!

LET'S GO LOOK AT SHOES.

CHECK OUT THE $400 SATIN PEACE SYMBOL WEDGIES! THEY'RE PERFECT WITH OUR $275 SHREDDED DENIMS!!

NIPPED-IN JACKETS... CINCHED DRESSES... BELTS GALORE! THIS YEAR WE CELEBRATE THE REAPPEARANCE OF THE WAIST!

OH, NO.

YES! LAST YEAR WE CELEBRATED THE REAPPEARANCE OF THE BUST AND THIS YEAR WE CELEBRATE THE REAPPEARANCE OF THE WAIST!

WHEN DO WE GET TO CELEBRATE THE REAPPEARANCE OF THE HIPS?

SORRY.

THERE'S NEVER A PARTY FOR THE ONE WHO REALLY NEEDS IT.

116

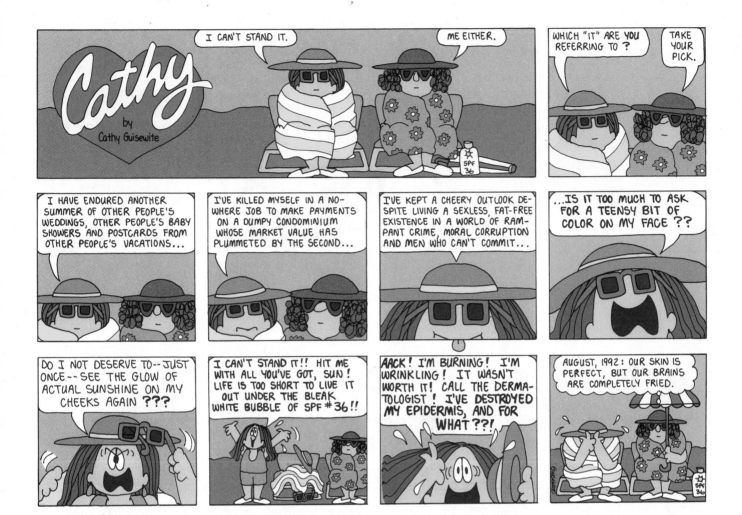

123

Panel 1: OUR GOWNS TAKE A YEAR TO ORDER. / I KNOW, BUT WHEN I GOT ENGAGED LAST FEBRUARY I COULDN'T ORDER A GOWN BECAUSE MY FIANCÉ WAS TOO PARANOID TO BUY A RING. — BRIDAL SALON

Panel 2: WHEN I GOT THE RING IN AUGUST, IT WAS TOO LATE TO ORDER A GOWN BECAUSE I WAS OBSESSED WITH HAVING THE WEDDING IN OCTOBER... ...WHEN WE TEMPORARILY BROKE UP IN OCTOBER IT WAS TOO LATE TO ORDER A GOWN BECAUSE MY MOTHER INSISTED ON A CHRISTMAS WEDDING.

Panel 3: WHEN HALF HIS RELATIVES QUIT SPEAKING OVER THE HOLIDAYS, WE HAD TO POSTPONE THE WEDDING AGAIN...BUT I'M BACK! I'VE TECHNICALLY BEEN IN THE GOWN MARKET FOR A YEAR, THE WEDDING'S SET FOR MARCH, **AND I WANT A DRESS!!**

Panel 4: OUR GOWNS TAKE A YEAR TO ORDER. / IS THERE ANY INDUSTRY LESS EQUIPPED TO CATER TO HUMAN RELATIONSHIPS? — BRIDAL SALON

Panel 5: I UNDERSTAND WHY YOU KEPT YOUR DISTANCE FROM ME THIS WEEK, IRVING...

Panel 6: THERE'S SO MUCH EMOTIONAL TENSION AROUND AN EVENT LIKE THIS...NO ONE'S LIFE CHANGES WITHOUT ALL OF OUR LIVES CHANGING.

Panel 7: CHARLENE AND SIMON'S WEDDING WILL HAVE A PROFOUND IMPACT ON ALL OF US! / THAT'S THIS WEEKEND? YOU'RE KIDDING.

Panel 8: IF MEN'S HAIR FALLS OUT, IT'S BECAUSE THERE'S NOTHING IN THERE FOR IT TO HOLD ONTO.

Panel 9: AACK! THE LINE! I'M AT THE LINE! I CAN SEE THE ACTUAL LINE!! / WHAT LINE, CATHY? — Congratula

Panel 10: HALF THE RELATIVES AT YOUR WEDDING ARE TRYING TO FIX ME UP, AND HALF AREN'T BECAUSE I LOOK TOO OLD. I'M AT THE EXACT BORDERLINE! THE LINE ON THE MAP!

Panel 11: ONE FOOT IS IN THE STATE OF DESIRABILITY AND ONE FOOT IS IN THE STATE OF DECAY! — Congrat

Panel 12: FIND THE PHOTOGRAPHER! I'M AN HISTORIC LANDMARK! / "MAID OF HONOR" MAY HAVE BEEN AN OVERSTATEMENT.

134

140

145

147

148

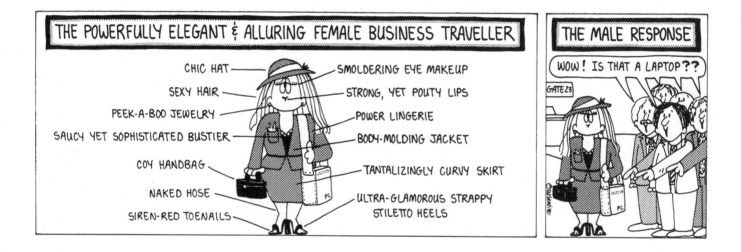

150

157

THE
END